Accounting for Freight

Steven M. Bragg

AccountingTools®

ISBN 978-1-64221-250-1

For more information about AccountingTools® products, visit our Web site at www.accountingtools.com.

Table of Contents

About the Author

Steven Bragg, CPA, has been the chief financial officer or controller of four companies, as well as a consulting manager at Ernst & Young. He received a master's degree in finance from Bentley College, an MBA from Babson College, and a Bachelor's degree in Economics from the University of Maine. He has been a two-time president of the Colorado Mountain Club, and is an avid alpine skier, mountain biker, and certified master diver. Mr. Bragg resides in Centennial, Colorado. He has written more than 300 books and courses, including *New Controller Guidebook*, *GAAP Guidebook*, and *Payroll Management*.

Steven maintains the accountingtools.com web site, which contains continuing professional education courses, the Accounting Best Practices podcast, and thousands of articles on accounting subjects.

Accounting for Freight

Introduction

The cost of freight plays a significant role in the financial statements of many businesses that deal in tangible goods. It may be added to the cost of inventory and fixed assets, or reported separately for lesser amounts, and may be billed through to customers – perhaps with a profit margin added to it. In this manual, we explore all aspects of the accounting for freight, including the treatment of freight-in and freight-out, its presentation in the financial statements, applicable controls, and more.

Types of Shipments

When goods are being shipped from a supplier to the buyer, the parties agree upon who will be billed for the associated freight charges. When a common carrier delivers the goods (which is the most common scenario), it issues a freight bill to either the supplier or the recipient.

> **Note:** A *common carrier* is a business that transports goods or people for other parties, and is responsible for any possible loss of the goods during transport. Its services are available to anyone in its coverage area that is willing to pay a fee. Examples of common carriers are air transport companies, trucking companies, and shipping firms.

Two key terms associated with freight are FOB shipping point and FOB destination. *FOB shipping point* is a contraction of the term "Free on Board Shipping Point." The term means that the buyer takes delivery of the goods being shipped to it by a supplier once the goods leave the supplier's shipping dock. Since the buyer takes ownership at the point of departure from the supplier's shipping dock, the supplier should record a sale at that point. The buyer should record an increase in its inventory at the same point, since the buyer is undertaking the risks and rewards of ownership, which occurs at the point of departure from the supplier's shipping dock. Also, under these terms, the buyer is responsible for the cost of shipping the goods to its facility. If the goods are damaged in transit, the buyer should file a claim with the insurance carrier, since the buyer has title to the goods during the period when the goods were damaged.

Realistically, it is quite difficult for the buyer to record a delivery at the shipping point, since this requires proper notification of shipment from the supplier. From a practical perspective, recognition of receipt is instead completed at the receiving dock of the buyer. Thus, a sale is recorded by the supplier when the shipment leaves the supplier's facility, and the receipt is recorded when it arrives at the buyer's facility. This means there is a difference between the legal terms of the arrangement and the typical accounting for it.

EXAMPLE

Absolution Corporation manufacturers pews for churches. It orders several thousand feet of oak boards from a supplier in Georgia, to be shipped to Absolution's production facility in Missouri under FOB shipping point terms. The supplier records the $28,000 sale of the goods as soon as the truck leaves its facility. Absolution receives no warning from the supplier that the goods have shipped, and so only records its receipt of the inventory three days later, when the boards arrive in Missouri. During inspection at the receiving dock, it is discovered that the top layer of boards was damaged while in transit. Since Absolution took ownership of the delivery as soon as it left the supplier's shipping dock, it files an insurance claim for recovery of the losses it suffered as a result of the damage.

FOB destination is a contraction of the term "Free on Board Destination." The term means that the buyer takes delivery of goods being shipped to it by a supplier once the goods arrive at the buyer's receiving dock. There are four variations on the FOB destination terms, which are as follows:

- *FOB destination, freight prepaid and allowed.* The seller pays and bears the freight charges, and owns the goods while they are in transit. Title passes at the buyer's location.
- *FOB destination, freight prepaid and added.* The seller pays the freight charges, but bills them to the buyer. The seller owns the goods while they are in transit. Title passes at the buyer's location.
- *FOB destination, freight collect.* The buyer pays the freight charges at the time of receipt, though the supplier still owns the goods while they are in transit.
- *FOB destination, freight collect and allowed.* The buyer pays for the freight costs, but deducts the cost from the supplier's invoice. The seller still owns the goods while they are in transit.

Thus, the key elements of all the variations on FOB destination terms are the physical location during transit at which title changes and who pays for the freight. If goods are damaged in transit, the seller should file a claim with the insurance carrier, since the seller has title to the goods during the period when the goods were damaged.

EXAMPLE

Apple Bespoke Confections (ABC) produces custom apple pies for its discerning customers. The main component of its products is (obviously) apples. It obtains them from Sunderland Orchards, which is located 300 miles away. The shipping terms used to deliver these apples is FOB destination, freight collect. On Monday morning, a common carrier collects a shipment of applies from Sunderland, and delivers them later that afternoon to ABC, where ABC pays all freight charges to the carrier at the receiving dock. Once the apples have been inspected, the ABC staff realizes that someone gained access to the applies while they were in transit (probably at a rest stop), and stole the contents of several crates of apples. Since Sunderland still owned the apples while they were in transit, it is responsible for filing a claim for the missing product.

As an additional consideration, it is quite common for the routing of goods to involve a mix of different types of transport, which is known as *intermodal transport*. For example, a Chinese supplier may load goods onto a container ship, which delivers the goods to a port, at which point the containers are loaded onto a train for transport to a rail spur in the middle of the country, where they are offloaded to a truck and delivered to the end customer. A single carrier will handle the logistics for intermodal transport, so that a company's transportation department only has to schedule a single transaction – the carrier handles the freight transfers among the different transport providers, and issues a single consolidated billing to the company.

Accounting for Freight-In

Freight-in is the cost associated with freight deliveries *into* an organization, and includes the costs of shipping and handling. Freight-in costs will be incurred when a delivery involves FOB shipping point terms. There are two ways to account for freight-in. One approach is to include it in the cost of inventory. If this path is followed and the associated goods are not immediately sold, then some of the freight-in cost will end up being capitalized into month-end inventory. This means that the cost will not be immediately charged to expense in a firm's income statement. Instead, the freight costs will appear in the balance sheet, within the inventory line item. Once the inventory items are sold, the associated freight cost is charged to expense. This approach is more complex for the accountant, since it requires one to charge freight costs to specific inventory items, or to the inventory account as a whole. Offsetting this annoyance is the ability to delay the recognition of some freight costs until a later period.

EXAMPLE

Milagro Industries purchases 50 industrial coffee grinders. It records $500 of inbound freight cost associated with the delivery of these motors, as noted in the following entry:

	Debit	Credit
Inventory (asset)	500	
Accounts payable (liability)		500

This transaction results in $10 of cost being added to each of the coffee grinders. In the same month, Milagro sells 30 of the coffee grinders to its customers. This means that $300 of the freight cost is charged to expense within the month, using the following entry:

	Debit	Credit
Cost of goods sold (expense)	300	
Inventory (asset)		300

The 20 remaining grinders are sold in the following month, at which point the remaining $200 of freight cost is charged to expense.

There are instances in which a business might incur an abnormally large freight cost, perhaps because a part needed to be air freighted in at the last moment due to a scheduling error. Abnormal expenses of this type are not to be added to inventory; instead, they should be charged to expense as incurred.

EXAMPLE

Rubens Trailers, producer of double-wide trailers for the rotund, finds that it has the wrong air conditioning units on hand, due to the mislabeling of the units currently in stock. In order to satisfy a customer that is expecting a delivery early in the following month, Rubens pays $1,000 to have a single unit air freighted to its manufacturing facility. This cost is classified as abnormal, and so should be charged to expense at once.

Another option is to charge the freight cost straight to expense as incurred. This approach works well if the amount of freight-in is relatively small. Also, it eliminates the need to charge freight costs to specific inventory items. The main downside is that freight costs are charged to expense somewhat more quickly than would be the case if these costs were to be added to the cost of inventory instead.

EXAMPLE

The Kris Kringle Christmas Shoppe manufactures Christmas ornaments. It uses a level manu-facturing schedule, so that production operations continue at a steady pace throughout the year. All of its sales are from September to November. The firm has historically purchased many of its raw materials from several suppliers located in Vietnam, which send the ordered items in container loads by ocean transport. The cost of freight-in is generally about $10,000 per month. Historically, Kris Kringle's accountant has charged this cost to expense as incurred. However, the company needs a working capital loan to support its production activities, and the bank is puzzled by the existence of this charge in months when there are no sales. It is so puzzled that the bank is considering not renewing the loan for next year. To ensure that the loan is renewed, the accountant elects to start charging freight costs to inventory, thereby delaying recognition of the associated expense until the sale of the ornaments during the September to November time period.

Despite the preceding example involving seasonal sales, it is generally much easier to charge the costs of freight-in to expense as these costs are incurred. Doing so can accelerate the recognition of freight expense somewhat, but for many companies, the amount of freight expense involved is relatively small. The main reason for an imme-diate charge off is to keep the cost of freight-in from mucking up the inventory rec-ords. It is just one more item that gets loaded into the bill of materials (for a standard costing system) or allocated to inventory through overhead, which increases the work load of the accounting staff. Also, keeping freight costs out of the inventory records reduces the work load of a firm's outside auditors, which may slightly reduce their annual audit fee.

A further reason for not including freight costs in inventory is the lower of cost or market analysis. This analysis is conducted periodically to see if the recorded cost of inventory items is higher than their fair market value; if so, the recorded cost must be reduced to the fair market value. It is possible that any freight costs assigned to spe-cific inventory items would be charged to expense as part of the mandated cost reduc-tion.

In short, and except in the case of seasonal sales, it generally makes more sense to charge the cost of freight-in relating to the delivery of inventory to expense as in-curred. Doing so simplifies the work of the accounting department.

Standard Costing and Freight-In

Standard costing is the practice of substituting an expected cost for an actual cost in the accounting records. Subsequently, variances are recorded to show the difference between the expected and actual costs. This approach represents a simplified alterna-tive to cost layering systems, such as the FIFO and LIFO methods, where large amounts of historical cost information must be maintained for inventory items held in stock.

Standard costing involves the creation of estimated (i.e., standard) costs for some or all activities within a company. The core reason for using standard costs is that there are a number of applications where it is too time-consuming to collect actual costs, so standard costs are used as a close approximation to actual costs. These standard cost amounts are stored within a *bill of materials*, which is a record of the raw materials, sub-assemblies, supplies, and freight costs used to construct a product. Since the cost of freight-in is included in a bill of lading, this presents the question of how to derive the most appropriate freight-in cost. Ideally, the cost chosen should represent the most likely per-unit freight cost that will actually be incurred. Issues to consider when deriving this amount are as follows:

- Whether the same part is being provided by more than one supplier. When this is the case, the distances, routings, and modes of transport may differ for each supplier, resulting in differing per-unit freight charges.
- Whether parts are being delivered in less-than-truckload (LTL) or full truckload quantities. LTL deliveries can be considerably more expensive on a per-unit basis that full truckload quantities.

EXAMPLE

Active Exercise Machines produces treadmills for the home exercise market. It uses a standard costing system to compile the cost of its various treadmill products. Its bill of materials includes a standard cost line item for each treadmill component, including the motor, front roller, rear roller, crossbars, handrail, console, walking belt, and footrails. It also includes a $37.15 line item for freight, which is the average freight charge incurred to acquire several of the parts included in the treadmill. The freight charge is based on the rates currently being charged to obtain parts from existing suppliers, assuming LTL deliveries.

Businesses routinely conduct variance analyses to spot any differences between standard and actual costs. The freight component of the bill of materials tends to cause more variances than other line items, because the other items are frequently contracted for under long-term purchasing agreements that lock in their price; this is less likely to be the case for freight rates.

> **Note:** Some companies prefer to roll freight costs into the overall cost of each component listed on a bill of materials. Doing so is easier than compiling freight costs separately, but the downside is that freight costs are then hidden in the bill of materials, and so are not readily subject to variance analysis.

The Application of Freight-In to Fixed Assets

When a business purchases a fixed asset, it should include in the cost of the asset all expenditures required to bring it to the condition and location intended for its use. This means that the cost of the freight required to transport an asset to its intended location should be capitalized into its cost. This has a direct impact on the expense recognition associated with the freight, since the freight will now be charged to expense as part of the periodic depreciation charges associated with the asset.

EXAMPLE

Lowry Locomotion purchases some heavy equipment, to be used in the construction of the turbo-diesel train engines for which it is famous. This is heavy and bulky equipment, so the cost of the freight required to bring the equipment to Lowry's factory is substantial, at $25,000. The equipment cost $975,000, so the total capitalized amount of the new asset is $1,000,000. Lowry's accounting staff plans to depreciate it over the next 10 years, after which the equipment will have no salvage value. This means that the annual depreciation charge on the equipment, including the capitalized cost of freight, will be $100,000.

The main financial reporting impact of capitalizing freight costs into fixed assets is that freight charges cannot be expensed as incurred. Instead, the recognition period can be quite prolonged, depending on the useful life of the relevant asset. In the preceding example, the $25,000 freight charge is only recognized at the rate of $2,500 per year.

If an invoice is received for freight charges relating to the transport of several fixed assets, then the freight charges should be apportioned among the assets. An easy way to do so is to apportion the cost based on the relative values of the assets, as noted in the following example.

EXAMPLE

Armadillo Industries purchases three injection molding machines of differing sizes for its plastic body armor production facility. The machines cost $300,000, $400,000, and $500,000. The freight charge to transport these machines to Armadillo's production facility is $30,000. The company's accountant elects to apportion the freight charge to the three machines based on their relative costs, resulting in the following calculation:

Machine	Unit Cost	Proportion of Total	Freight Allocation	Total Cost
1	$300,000	25%	$7,500	$307,500
2	400,000	33%	10,000	410,000
3	500,000	42%	12,500	512,500
	$1,200,000	100%	$30,000	$1,230,000

Fixed assets may be updated from time to time. If these updates prolong the life of the asset or enhance its functionality, then the cost of the updates is capitalized – along with any freight costs incurred to ship any associated materials to the organization. Conversely, if an update does *not* prolong the life of an asset or enhance its functionality, then the cost of the update is charged to expense in the current period – along with any freight costs incurred.

Accounting for Freight-Out

Freight-out is the cost associated with freight deliveries *out of* an organization, and includes the costs of shipping and handling. Freight-out costs will be incurred when a delivery involves FOB destination terms. In this situation, the seller is responsible for the costs incurred to move goods to the destination specified by the buyer.

The most common way to account for freight-out is to charge it to expense in the period incurred. A possible issue is the timing of the expense recognition. Under the *matching principle*, all costs associated with a sale are supposed to be recognized in the same period as the sale, so that the complete profit or loss associated with the transaction can be viewed in one period. However, an invoice for outbound freight might not arrive from the carrier until the next month, which means that the expense recognition is incorrectly delayed.

Given the amount of expense involved, many companies do not bother to accrue the cost of freight-out in the correct period. Instead, they wait for the freight invoice to arrive, and then record it in whatever period that happens to be. From a practical perspective, it may only make sense to accrue freight expense when the related (and as-yet unreceived) carrier invoice is expected to be quite large. For all other freight invoices, the amounts involved are too small to make it worth the effort to match up every shipment with every freight billing to see which invoices have not yet been received, and estimate what the invoice amount should be.

EXAMPLE

Grouch Electronics sells home theater systems, and ships these systems to its customers for free. It sells a massive $150,000 system to a Wall Street tycoon, for which the cost of the system components is $140,000, so it initially appears that the firm earned a profit of $10,000 on the deal. However, the associated freight billing did not arrive until the next month; this $2,000 charge is applied in the following month, after company management had already completed its profit-by-customer reports. Therefore, management does not see that its profit on the deal was reduced by 20% because of the late freight billing.

Tip: If the company's auditors insist that the company accrue freight expenses, the easiest way to do so is to simply delay closing the books at the end of the year, until all carrier invoices have been received. The closing process is usually delayed somewhat at year-end anyways, due to the large number of additional accounting tasks to be completed.

Another issue with freight-out is what to do if the shipper is re-billing the freight charge to the customer. The choices are to either treat the billing as a form of revenue, or to offset the billing against the freight-out expense. Freight-out billings to customers should only be treated as revenue when doing so is the primary revenue-generating activity of the shipping entity. In this situation, freight revenue should be recorded in a separate revenue account, so that management can clearly see how much revenue is being generated by this activity. And, since freight revenue is being separately recorded, then so too should the associated freight expense. Doing so makes it easier to determine the amount of profit generated by these freight billings.

EXAMPLE

Simon's Air Freight (SAF) is in the business of transporting goods for its customers. It focuses on the delivery of temperature-sensitive vaccines to out-of-the-way locations, which calls for the transport of refrigerated storage containers to short-length dirt runways, using twin-engine and single-engine propeller planes. It transports a new HIV vaccine to a number of villages in the hinterlands of Ghana, and charges the sponsoring non-profit entity a freight charge of $4,000 for this service. Since SAF is in the business of generating freight revenue, this billing should be recorded in a separate revenue account. It is not offset against any related freight transport costs.

When the billing of freight is *not* the primary revenue-generating activity of the shipping entity, then any billed freight amount should instead be offset against the freight expense line item. The result should be quite a small freight expense. Also, if the shipper is adding a profit margin to the freight that it is charging to buyers, then the freight expense line item could easily be a negative figure.

EXAMPLE

Albatross Flight Systems constructs GPS systems for drones, and ships them to customers all over the world. It adds a 20% markup to the freight cost it incurs to each of these deliveries. In its most recent quarter of operations, the company incurred $8,000 of freight-out charges from various carriers, and billed its customers $9,600 in freight charges (calculated as $8,000 in freight costs × 1.2).

Albatross is not primarily in the business of generating revenue from its freight billings, so it should not record these billings as revenue. Instead, it records the following entry for the first quarter (assuming that all freight billings were recorded at once, which is unlikely to be the case):

	Debit	Credit
Freight expense (expense)	8,000	
Accounts payable (liability)		8,000

It then bills the buyers of GPS units for the freight as part of its invoices, for which the freight-related part of the entry is as follows:

	Debit	Credit
Accounts receivable (asset)	9,600	
Freight expense (expense)		9,600

The result is a negative freight expense of $1,600 for the quarter.

The Reserve for Freight Bad Debts

When freight charges are to be billed to customers, a reasonable question to ask is whether it makes sense to set up a reserve for freight bad debts. When a business uses the accrual basis of accounting, it commonly sets up an allowance for doubtful accounts, which is a contra account[1] that is paired with and offsets the accounts receivable asset account. When combined, the net amount of these two accounts equals the amount of receivables that management expects to actually collect.

> **Note:** The *accrual basis of accounting* employs the concept of recording revenues when earned and expenses as incurred. It is the standard approach to recording transactions in all larger businesses.

The balance in the allowance for doubtful accounts is usually derived by one of two methods. The more labor-intensive approach is to identify which specific invoices are unlikely to be paid, based on input from the collections staff. The other approach is to reserve an amount that equals the firm's historical bad debt percentage. This percentage can be refined by applying a historical bad debt percentage to each 30-day bucket of invoices listed in the organization's accounts receivable aging report. For example, a 2% bad debt percentage is applied to invoices that are up to 30 days old, a 5% rate to those invoices in the 31-60 day range, and a 25% rate to those invoices that are over 60 days old, on the assumption that older invoices are more likely to become bad debts.

It is not necessary to set up a separate reserve for freight bad debts, since the likelihood of their not being paid is already recognized within the allowance for doubtful accounts. However, the reserve can be made more precise by identifying those customers that are more likely to short pay the freight portion of a billing, or not pay it at all. Applying this knowledge to the allowance may result in a slightly higher reserve balance.

---

[1] A contra account offsets the balance in another, related account with which it is paired. Contra accounts appear in the financial statements directly below their paired accounts. Sometimes the balances in the two accounts are merged for presentation purposes, so that only a net amount is presented.

EXAMPLE

Luminescence Corporation operates a floodlight manufacturing facility. Its customers are mostly smaller hardware stores that are located in small towns and cities. The financial health of these customers tends to be rather poor, so Luminescence experiences a high bad debt rate. It also charges its customers for the cost of delivering floodlights to them, which several customers refuse to pay, even though they pay the rest of the invoices issued to them. The company uses the accrual basis of accounting, and so maintains an allowance for doubtful accounts to recognize expected bad debt levels. To derive the reserve, the accounting department applies an increasing bad debt percentage to the unpaid invoices in each successive 30-day time bucket in the firm's aged accounts receivable report. In addition, the department then conducts a manual review of open invoices and highlights those issued to customers that have historically not paid the freight portion of their invoices. The freight stated on these invoices is then compiled and added to the reserve. In the most recent period, this resulted in an allowance of $42,000, of which $40,000 was calculated from historical bad debt percentages, and $2,000 was derived from an analysis of freight billings that were unlikely to be paid.

Tip: When customers short pay the freight portion of an invoice (or do not pay it at all), be sure to factor this amount into the calculation of profitability by customer. A customer that persistently does not pay this portion of an invoice may generate a significantly lower profit than expected.

Presentation of Freight Expenses

Freight expenses – of both the freight-in and freight-out varieties – should be reported within the cost of goods sold section of the income statement. This is because freight is only incurred to bring raw materials or completed goods into a business (freight-in) or to ship goods to buyers (freight-out), both of which are part of the core revenue-generating activities of a business.

Depending on the business, freight costs as a percentage of sales may be so low that they can be aggregated into the "Other Cost of Goods Sold" line item, rather than being stated in a separate line item. In cases where freight expenses are reported separately on the income statement and the balance is negative (as may be the case when freight billed to customers at a profit is offset against freight costs), it can make sense to explain the reason for the negative balance in the footnotes accompanying the financial statements. For example:

> The company reported freight expense of -$12,400 in the last quarter. The negative balance reported was due to the billing of freight-out to customers with a profit margin applied. The final balance was comprised of freight-out expenses incurred of $82,800 and freight-out billings of $95,200.

Some businesses prefer to list the cost of freight within the expenses of the sales department. This treatment is not recommended, since it implies that freight is part of the general, selling, and administrative functions of a business, which is usually not the case.

Analysis of Freight-in Charges

When the freight cost associated with bringing materials into a buyer facility is quite large, it can make sense for an analyst to periodically review it, and report findings back to management regarding the drivers of freight charges. Here are some issues that can cause the amount of freight expense to vary:

- *Rate changes.* Freight costs will vary over time, based on the costs incurred by freight operators. In particular, the cost of fuel can move markedly over just a few months. Also, changes in supply and demand can dramatically alter shipper rates. For example, the shipping rates associated with oil deliveries from the Middle East declined dramatically during the 2020 pandemic, when the demand for oil suddenly deteriorated.
- *Rush deliveries.* A production facility may have a scheduling or excessive scrap problem, and runs out of certain raw materials. If so, it may need to air freight the required materials to its facility on short notice. To be most useful, this analysis should state the specific scrap problem or scheduling error that triggered each rush delivery, so that management can use it to resolve the underlying issue.
- *Supplier locations.* The purchasing staff routinely alters the mix of suppliers from which materials are procured. This will result in different distances traveled to bring goods from a supplier to the company. For example, a business may elect to switch its sourcing from a local supplier to one located in Vietnam. If so, the freight cost will skyrocket, though this is presumably offset by the reduced unit costs of the goods being acquired.
- *Load size.* A business can obtain better freight rates when it purchases in full truckload quantities, and worse LTL rates for partial truckloads. Thus, a drop in purchasing volumes can trigger an inordinately large increase in freight charges, and vice versa.
- *New carriers.* A business might have inadvertently used a freight carrier with which it does not have a volume discount. This should be a relatively rare circumstance, since all transport arrangements should originate with a scheduling group that controls which carriers are used.

Evidence of Excessive Freight Charges

Someone analyzing a business might want to delve into its freight charges in order to gain a better understanding of the firm's overall performance. For example, this could be important for the prospective purchaser of a business, who wants to see if the organization has been using excessive freight charges to artificially enhance selected performance metrics. Thus, a business could improve its inventory turnover figure by maintaining excessively low inventory balances and then paying extra to have raw materials delivered through an overnight delivery service. To see if this is happening, track the cost of incoming freight in conjunction with the raw materials turnover ratio.

Similarly, a business can try to boost its on-time delivery percentage by paying excessive amounts to obtain merchandise on short notice, which it then ships through to its customers. To see if this is the case, track the cost of incoming freight in conjunction with the on-time delivery percentage.

EXAMPLE

The management of Medusa Medical (maker of questionable snake oil remedies) decides to adjust the firm's marketing strategy to focus on two-day deliveries to its customers. To support this strategy, it creates a generous bonus plan for employees that pays them if the one-day target is met for at least 95% of all customer orders. The problem is that management did not commit a sufficient amount of working capital funding to ensure that the firm could maintain enough inventory to fulfill orders on such short notice. Therefore, in order to meet the on-time delivery goal, employees contract with suppliers to drop ship[2] products directly to customers, using overnight delivery services – with all freight charges billed to the company. As a result, the company meets its on-time delivery target, but also generates a loss when its freight costs quadruple.

In both of the preceding scenarios, the main indicator is persistent, large billings from overnight delivery services. An indirect indicator is employee performance plans that excessively reward staff for achieving aggressive inventory turnover and/or on-time delivery percentages. These plans will present a strong temptation for employees to use overnight delivery services to provide a caffeinated boost to reported performance levels.

Controls Over Freight

The cost of freight can be relatively difficult to control, as can the cost recoveries achieved by billing freight through to customers. We discuss these issues in the following sub-sections.

Controls Over Freight-In

There are several controls over the cost of freight. One of the most essential is the separation of duties. This means that an employee who is responsible for obtaining freight estimates should not be the person making the final carrier selection, or paying the freight invoice. Otherwise, someone responsible for all of these activities could enter into an agreement with a carrier, where the carrier overcharges the party contracting its services and then pays a kickback to the person who approved the arrangement.

A key control is to ensure that all instructions and payment responsibilities have been properly negotiated prior to creating a purchase order for submission to a supplier. Clarifying this information up front allows the buyer to avoid the incurrence of excessive costs and inefficiencies in the routing of deliveries that might otherwise occur due to miscommunication.

---

[2] Drop shipping is the practice of having suppliers ship goods directly to one's customers.

> **Tip:** It can make sense to insist on directly paying for all freight charges, rather than being billed for it by the supplier. Since the party responsible for paying freight charges has control over the shipment routing, this allows the buyer to control both the routing and mode of transport, while also avoiding freight billings from the supplier that might have a profit margin built into them.

Another approach is to periodically review the freight rates being charged to the company for both freight-in and freight-out. These rates will vary substantially based on a variety of factors, such as the timing of deliveries, whether a full or partial truckload is to be used, and the amount of freight volume the organization has with the freight carrier in question. These variables can make it difficult to discern whether a carrier has increased its rates. Nonetheless, it can make sense to closely track the rates being charged on standard freight hauls on a trend line, to detect pricing changes. For example, a furniture manufacturer obtains all of its maple from a Georgia sawmill, which is delivered in a standard monthly truckload. Since the size and routing of the delivery are standard, the manufacturer is in a good position to track freight rates on an ongoing basis.

Another control is to hire a freight auditing firm to review the company's freight billings and spot instances of excessive rates being charged. This is a useful approach when the auditing firm charges a percentage of all recoveries for its efforts, so that the company incurs no net cost from engaging the services of the auditing firm.

Controls Over Freight-Out

There are several controls over the billings for freight that a company charges to its customers. One option is to periodically have the internal audit department compare the actual freight rates paid to ship goods to customers to the prices charged to customers for those deliveries. If this review uncovers any instances where the costs incurred are greater than the revenues billed, then the firm needs to revise its billing procedures to ensure that it at least breaks even on its outbound freight billings.

> **Tip:** When reviewing freight rates, be sure to compare the actual costs incurred for overnight deliveries to the amounts charged to customers. Overnight freight companies charge very high rates, which may not be properly reflected in the company's freight rates to customers.

When freight is billed to customers, the amount being billed may have been listed on the originating sales order, or is derived from a standard freight table, or is listed by the shipping manager on the forwarded bill of lading. No matter which method is used, the invoicing software should contain an automatic data validation feature, where an invoice cannot be completed unless a freight billing amount is included.

A more indirect control over freight billings is to routinely report to management the profits generated from sales to each customer. Doing so may highlight instances in which agreements to not bill customers for freight have led to inordinately low profit margins. Once management understands the impact of these arrangements, it may be more willing to bill customers for freight costs, or drop those customers who refuse to accept these charges.

General Controls Over Freight

Since the accounting treatment varies depending on whether a freight charge is for freight-in or freight-out, it makes sense to build in a control that flags the nature of each charge. One approach is to task the shipping and receiving staff with identifying these charges, since this group is in the best position to know. A lesser option is to assign all freight-out to a single carrier, and set up its vendor account in the accounting system with a default charge code that identifies its billings as freight-out. This is a lesser option, because the carrier might actually be involved in deliveries *to* the business, making it more difficult to determine which of its billings to the firm are for freight-in or freight-out.

Summary

The accounting for freight-in and freight-out is relatively straightforward. What is perhaps more important is how to maintain a proper degree of control over it. A thoughtfully-applied system of controls should be able to spot instances of over-billings by freight carriers, as well as cases in which freight was not billed through to customers, was billed at the wrong rate, or was not collected from them. Paying attention to these details can trigger a noticeable increase in the profitability of a business.

Glossary

A

Accrual basis of accounting. The concept of recording revenues when earned and expenses as incurred.

B

Bill of materials. A record of the raw materials, sub-assemblies, supplies, and freight costs used to construct a product.

C

Common carrier. A business that transports goods or people for other parties, and is responsible for any possible loss of the goods during transport.

Contra account. An account that offsets the balance in another, related account with which it is paired.

D

Drop shipping. The practice of having suppliers ship goods directly to one's customers.

F

Freight-in. Freight costs incurred by a purchaser.

Freight-out. The cost associated with freight deliveries *out of* an organization.

M

Matching principle. The concept that all costs associated with a sale are supposed to be recognized in the same period as the sale.

Index